I0815333

DIRTY HEALTH CARE JOBS

Kenny Abdo

Fly!
An Imprint of Abdo Zoom
abdobooks.com

abdobooks.com

Published by Abdo Zoom, a division of ABDO, P.O. Box 398166, Minneapolis, Minnesota 55439. Copyright © 2026 by Abdo Consulting Group, Inc. International copyrights reserved in all countries. No part of this book may be reproduced in any form without written permission from the publisher. Fly!™ is a trademark and logo of Abdo Zoom.

Printed in the United States of America, North Mankato, Minnesota.
052025
092025

Photo Credits: AdobeStock, Alamy, Getty Images, Shutterstock
Production Contributors: Kenny Abdo, Jennie Forsberg, Grace Hansen
Design Contributors: Candice Keimig, Neil Klinepier, Colleen McLaren

Library of Congress Control Number: 2024947690

Publisher's Cataloging-in-Publication Data

Names: Abdo, Kenny, author.
Title: Dirty health care jobs / by Kenny Abdo
Description: Minneapolis, Minnesota : Abdo Zoom, 2026 | Series: Dirty work | Includes online resources and index.
Identifiers: ISBN 9781098288716 (lib. bdg.) | ISBN 9781098289416 (ebook) | ISBN 9781098289768 (Read-to-me ebook)
Subjects: LCSH: Sanitation--Juvenile literature. | Careers--Juvenile literature. | Health care facilities--Juvenile literature. | Medical waste--Juvenile literature. | Medical and sanitary affairs--Juvenile literature.
Classification: DDC 331.70--dc23

TABLE OF CONTENTS

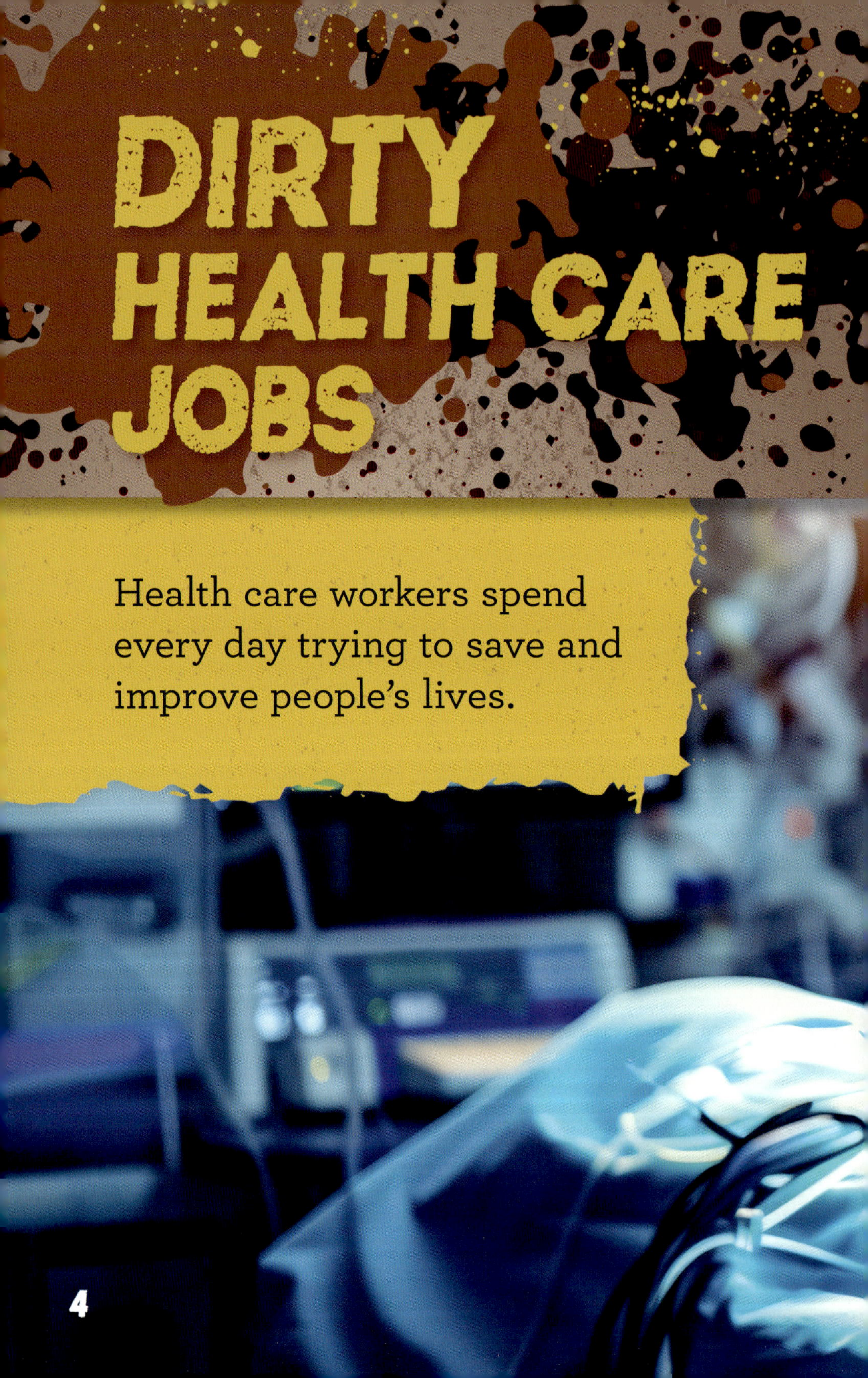

DIRTY HEALTH CARE JOBS

Health care workers spend every day trying to save and improve people's lives.

THE DIRT

Health care requires dealing with the messier side of life. Nurses, doctors, and **technicians** see blood, **infections**, and other unpleasant things daily.

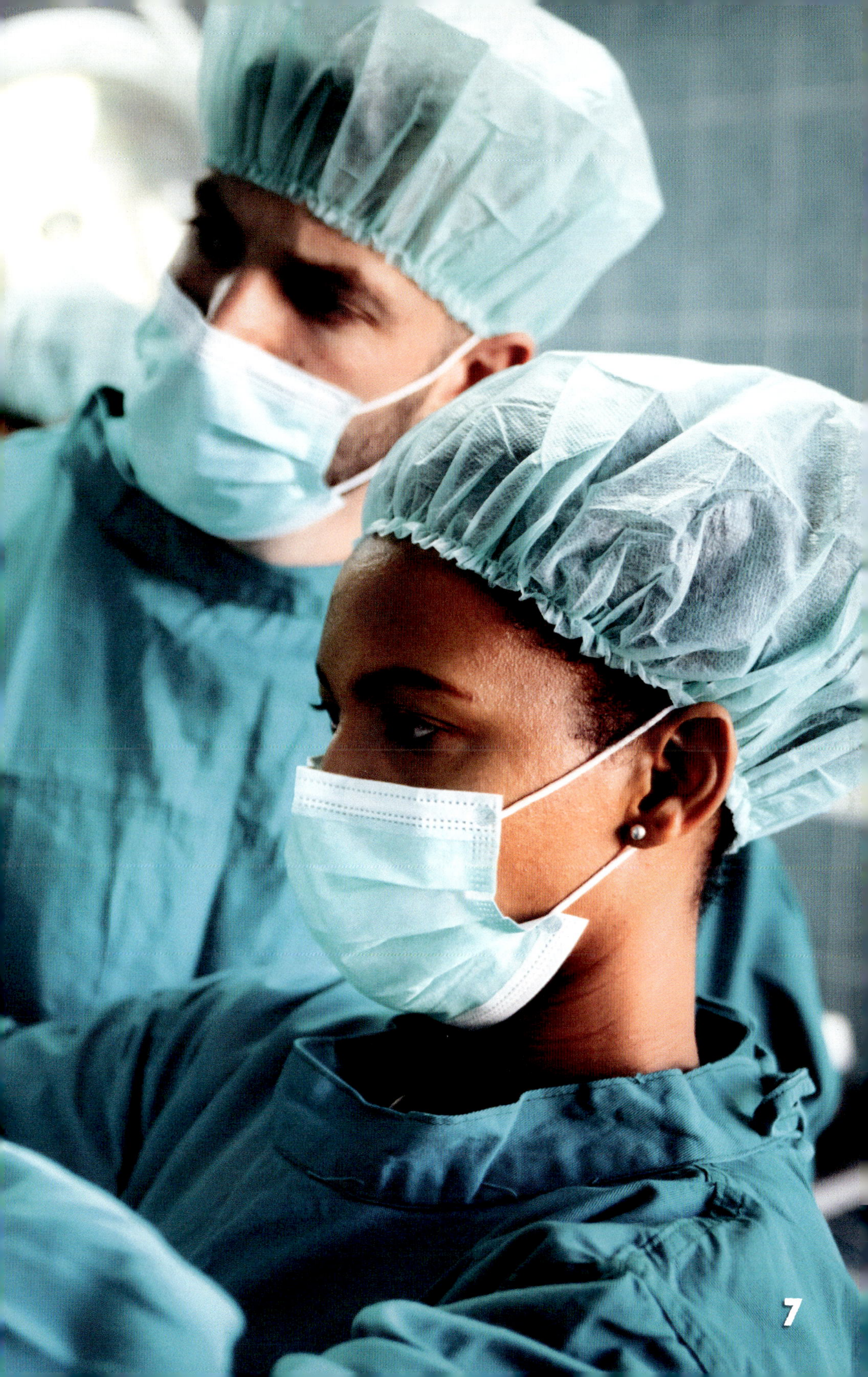

These jobs may seem germy and unappealing, but they are needed to save lives. Health care workers need a lot of *patience* when taking on their task!

THE WORK

Phlebotomists draw blood for tests and donations. They insert needles and handle blood bags. Occasionally, there are patients who get woozy when they see needles and blood. Phlebotomists have to be ready for any situation!

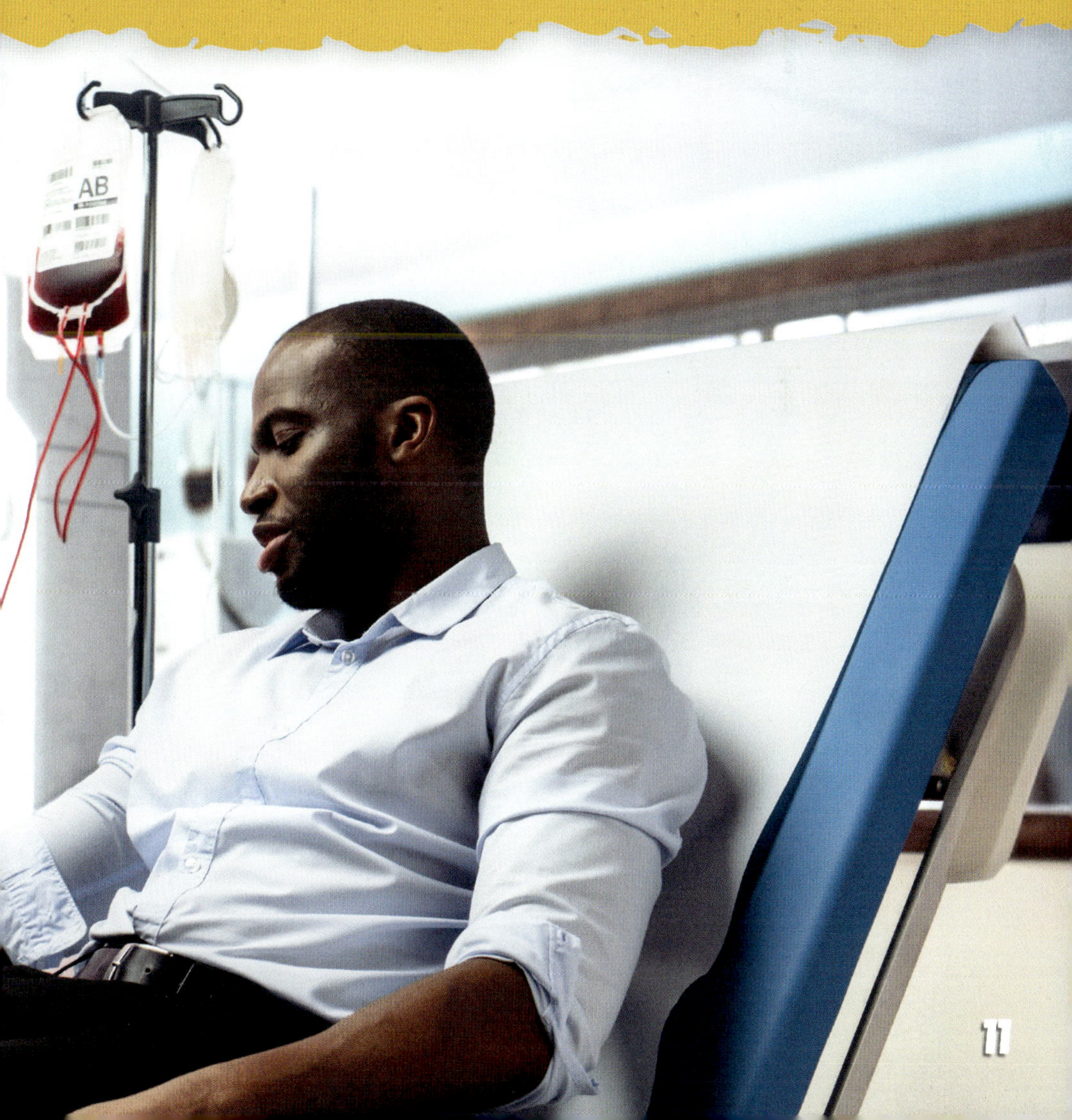

Medical waste disposal workers safely remove **biohazardous** materials. These materials include used syringes, bandages, and surgical materials. Workers follow strict safety **protocols** to handle the waste properly.

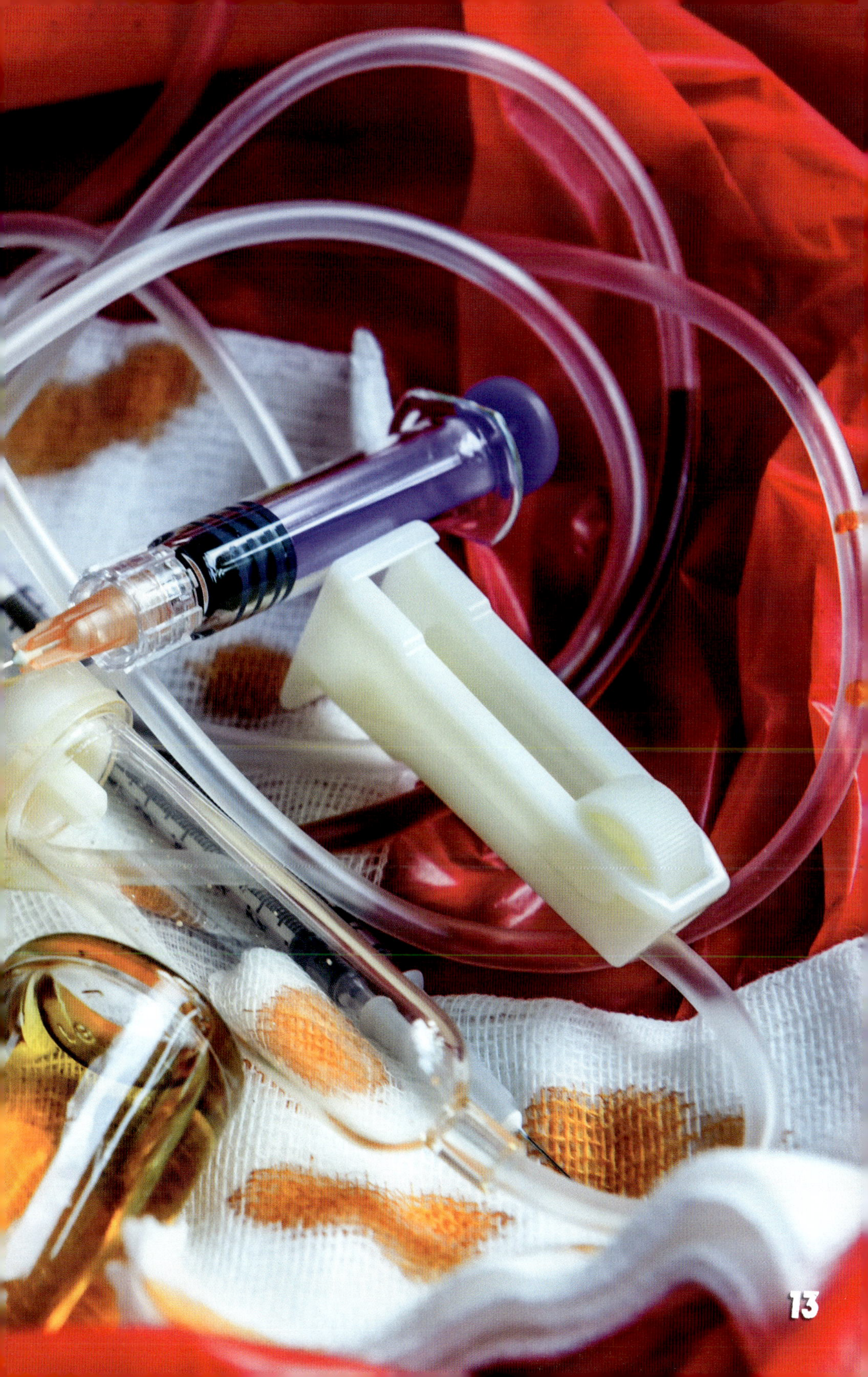

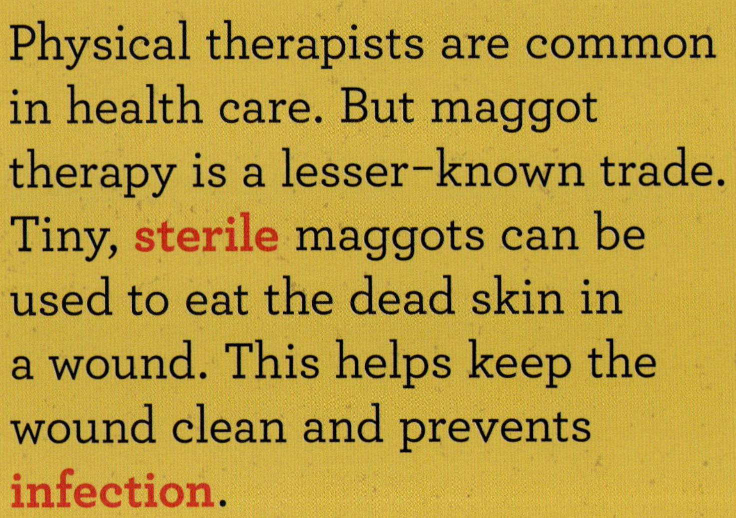

Physical therapists are common in health care. But maggot therapy is a lesser-known trade. Tiny, **sterile** maggots can be used to eat the dead skin in a wound. This helps keep the wound clean and prevents **infection**.

200
150

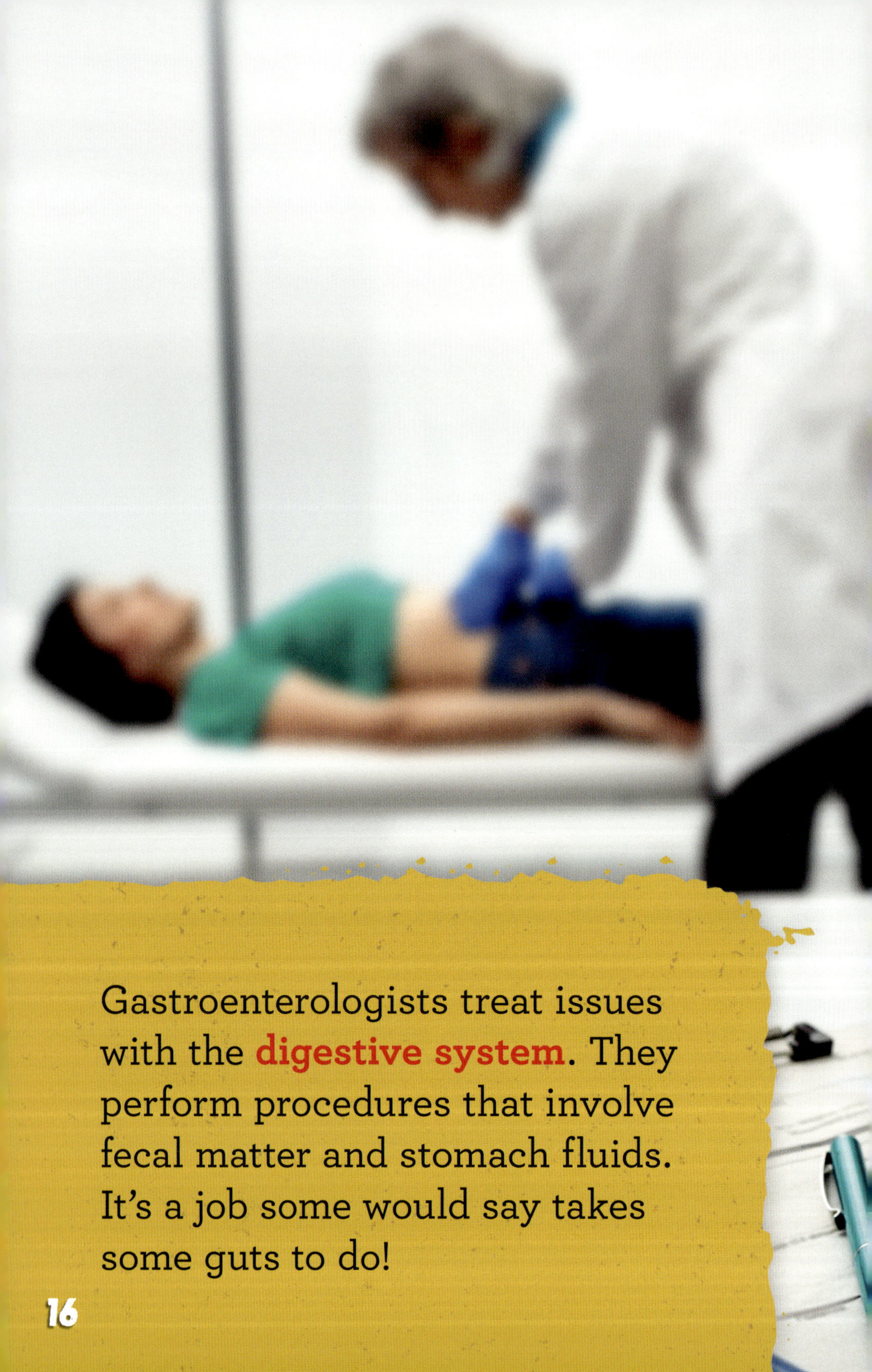

Gastroenterologists treat issues with the **digestive system**. They perform procedures that involve fecal matter and stomach fluids. It's a job some would say takes some guts to do!

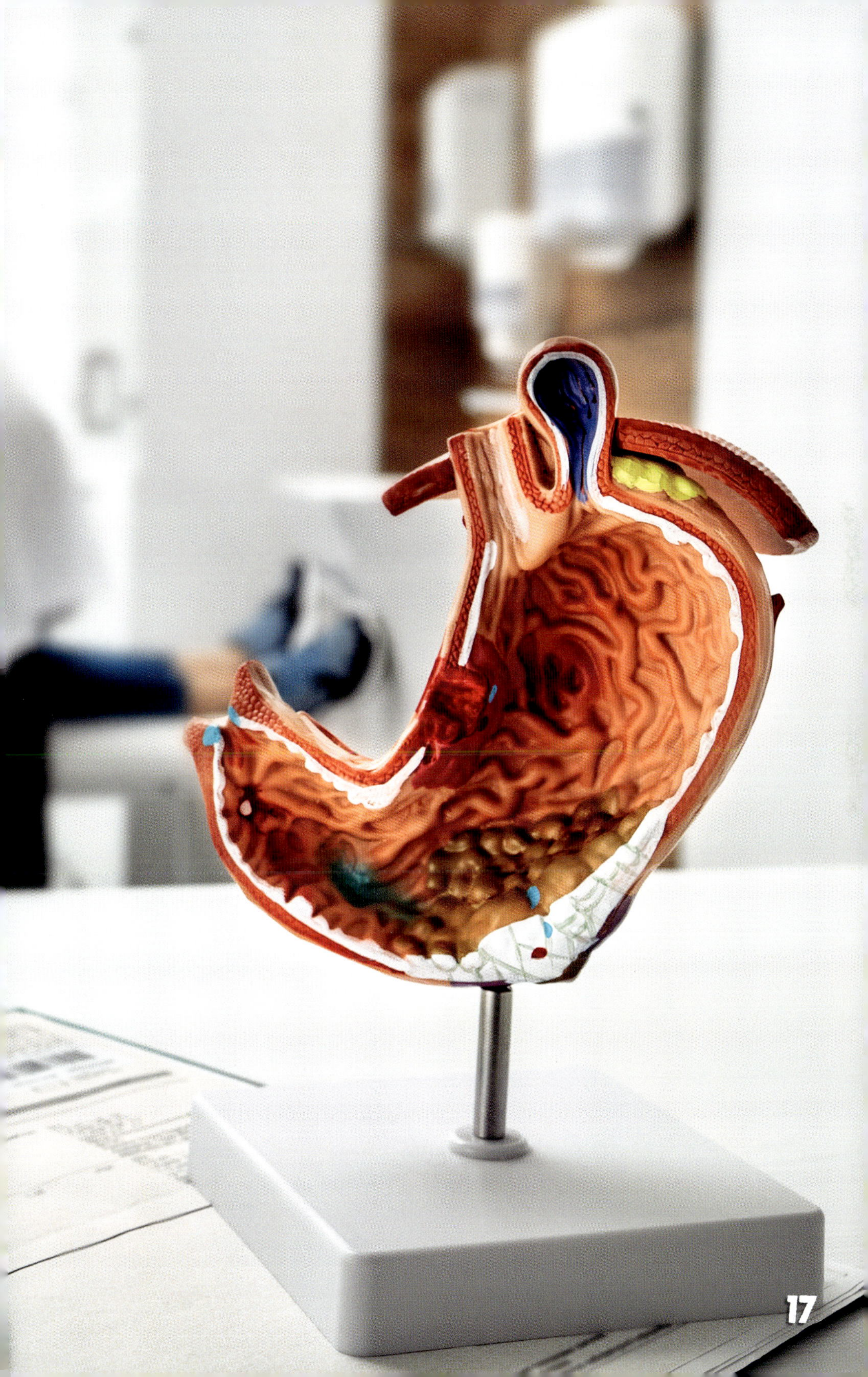

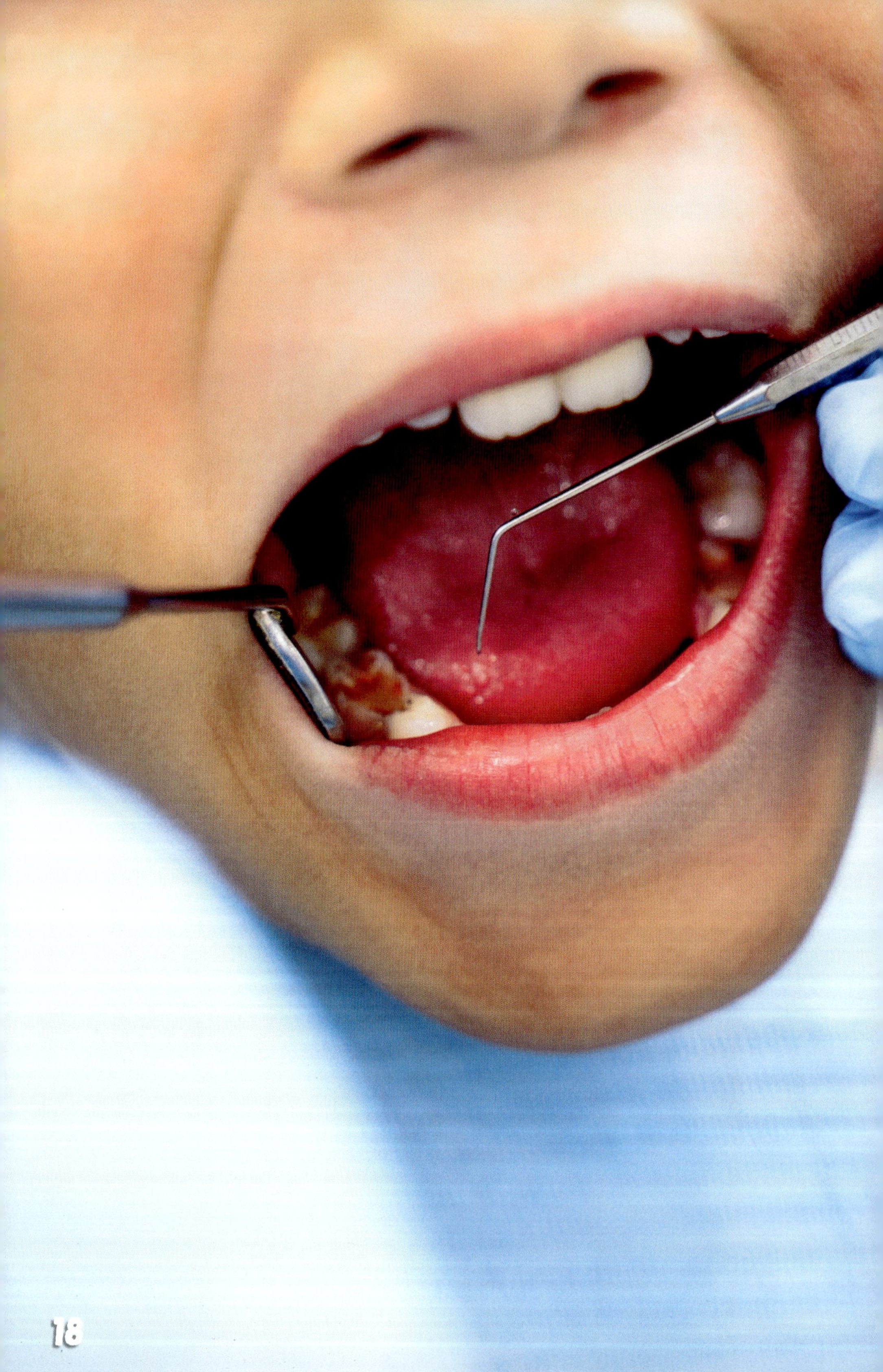

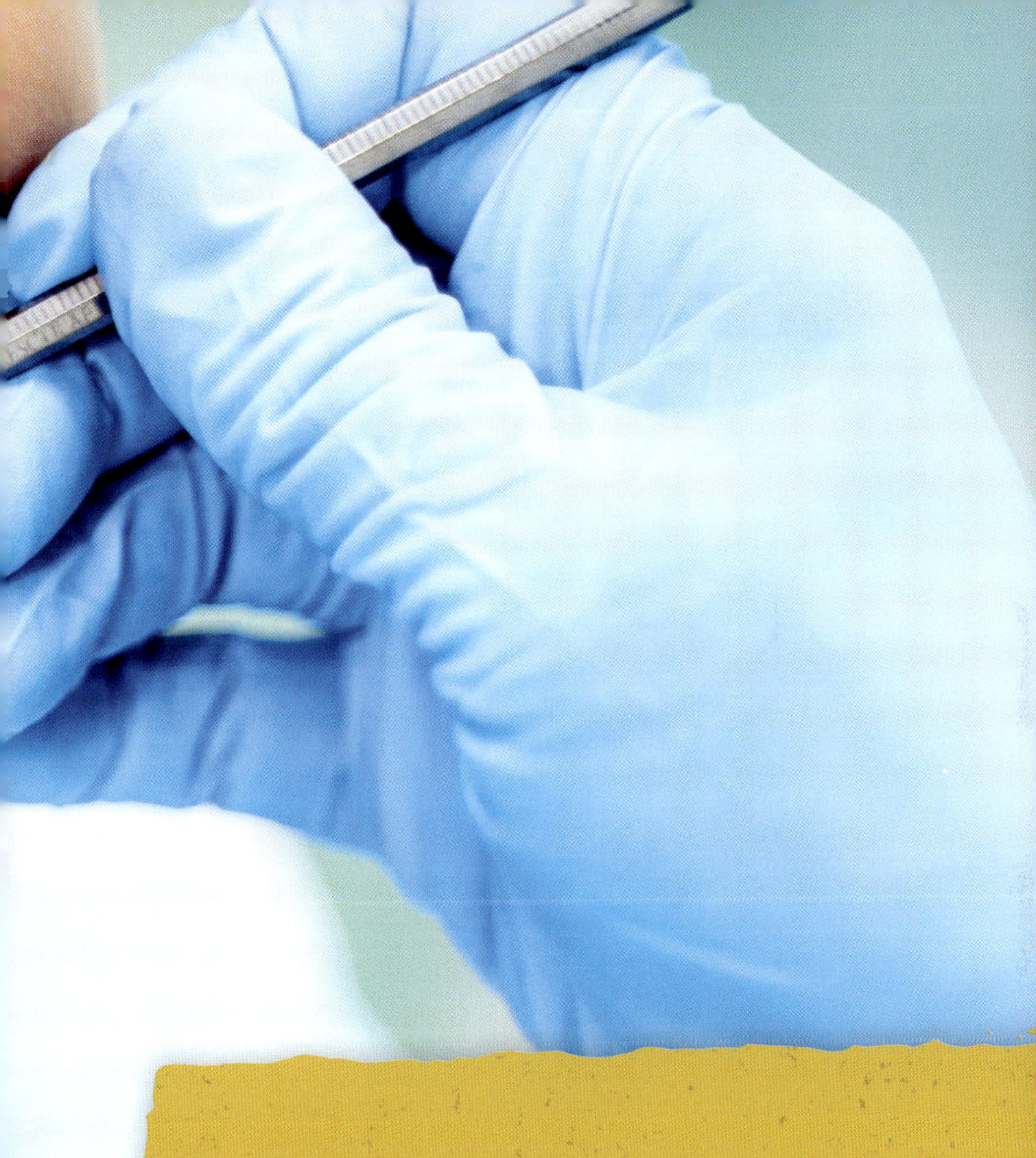

Dentists improve your smile and health. They fix problems such as bad breath, **plaque**, and **infections**. Their job is tough and requires a strong stomach and breath mints!

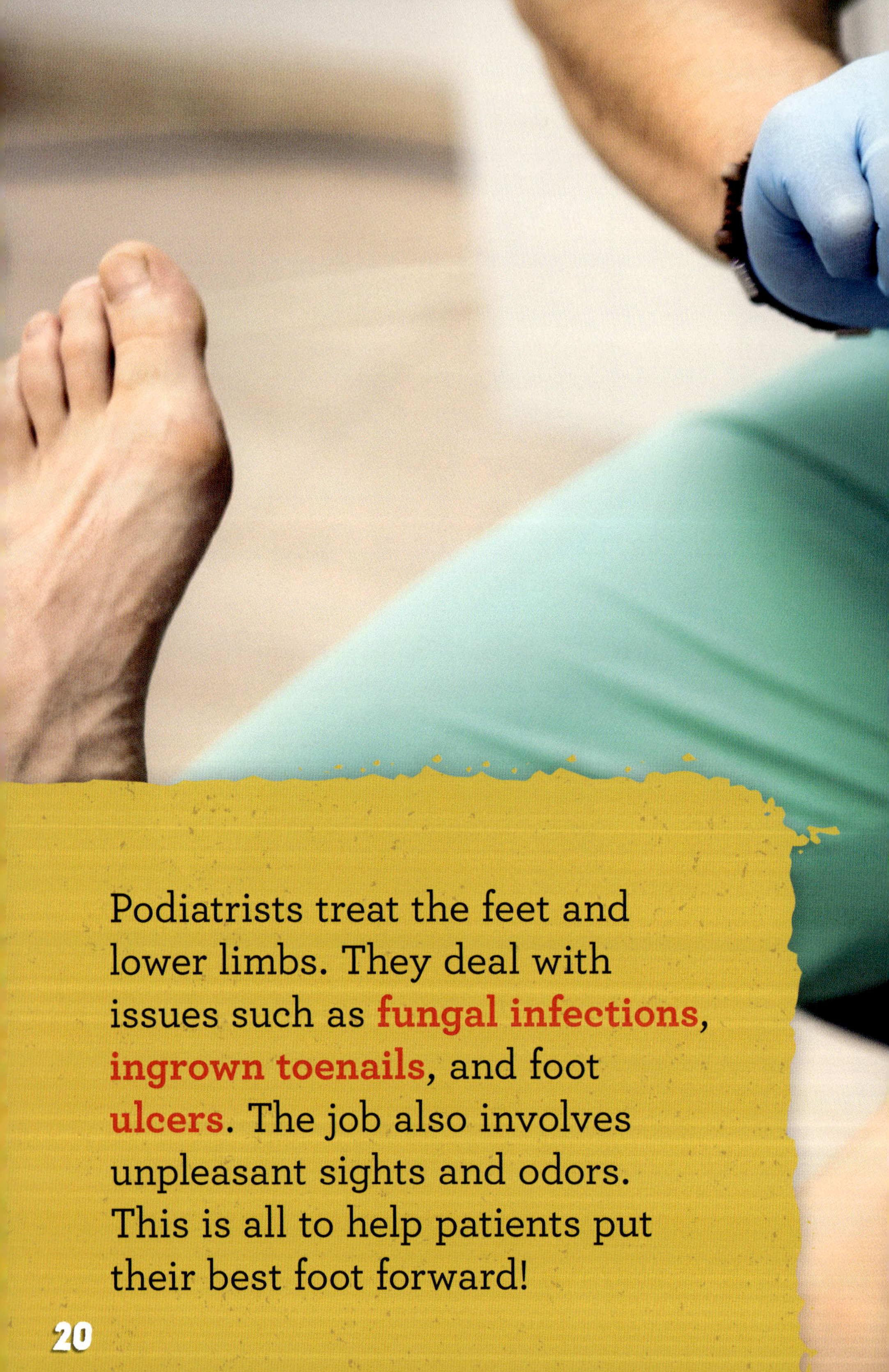

Podiatrists treat the feet and lower limbs. They deal with issues such as **fungal infections**, **ingrown toenails**, and foot **ulcers**. The job also involves unpleasant sights and odors. This is all to help patients put their best foot forward!

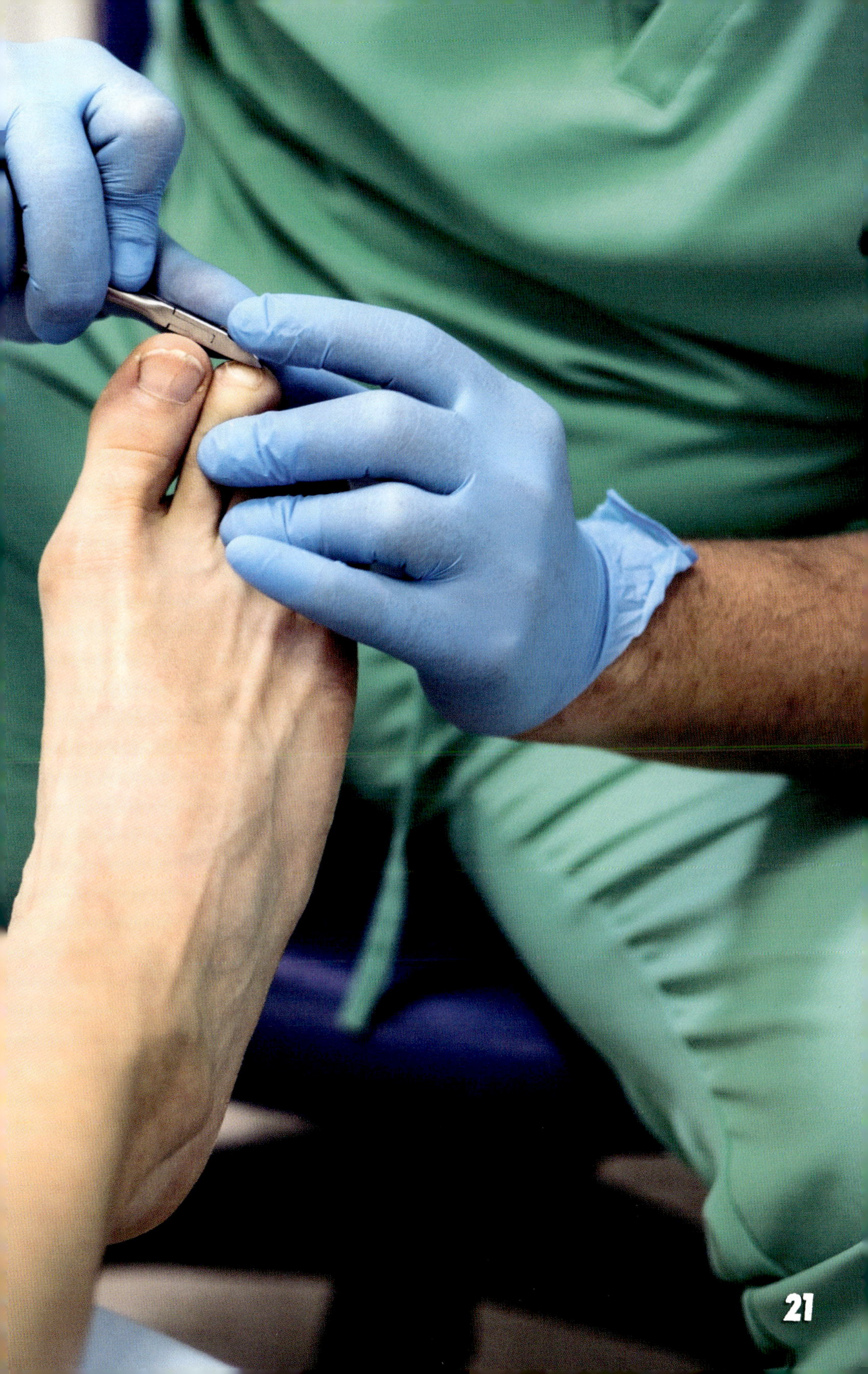

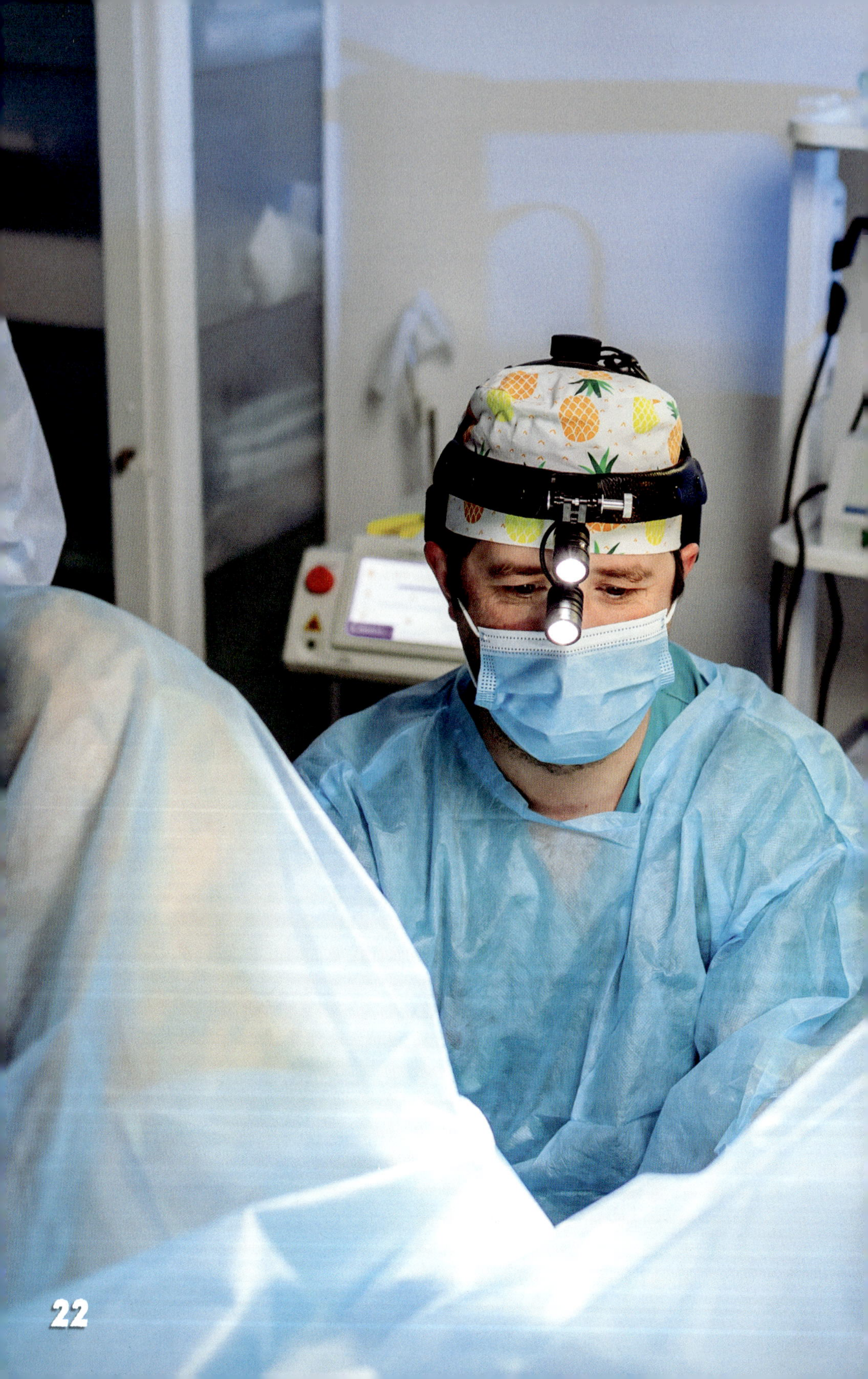

Proctologists treat issues in the lower **digestive** tract. They treat certain diseases and remove growths to keep people more comfortable. Patients do not want to be *behind* on their appointments!

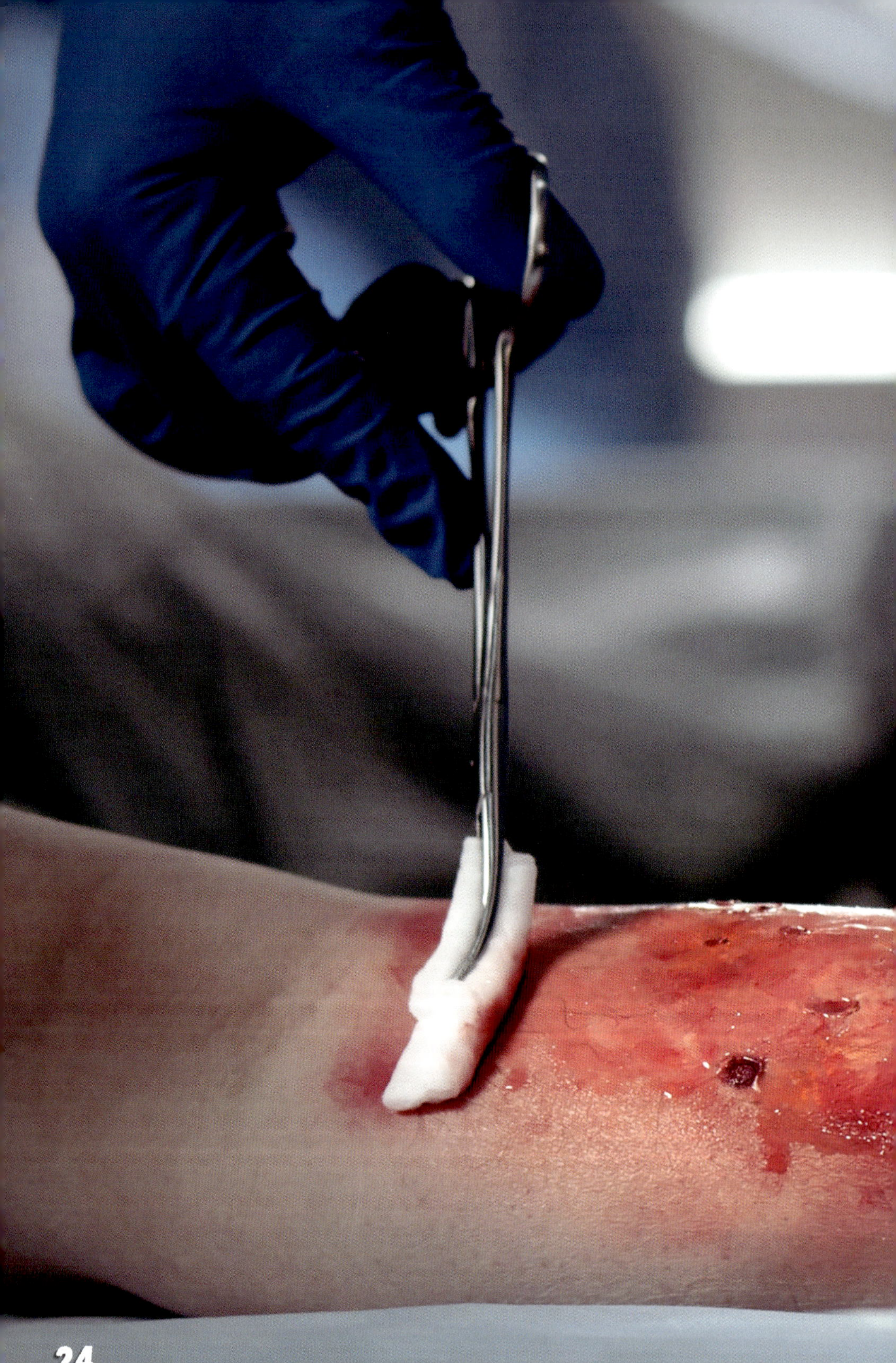

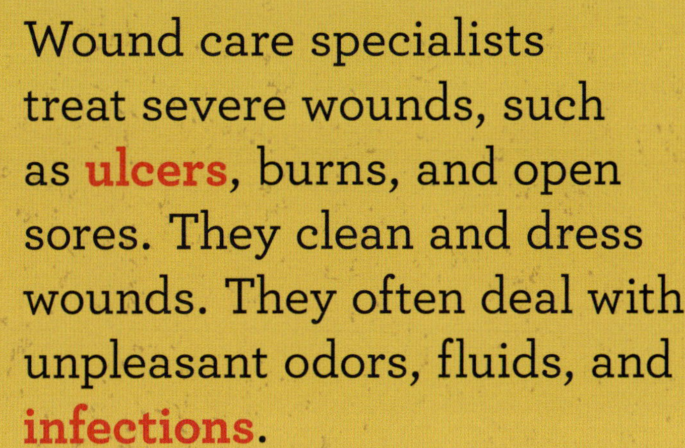

Wound care specialists treat severe wounds, such as **ulcers**, burns, and open sores. They clean and dress wounds. They often deal with unpleasant odors, fluids, and **infections**.

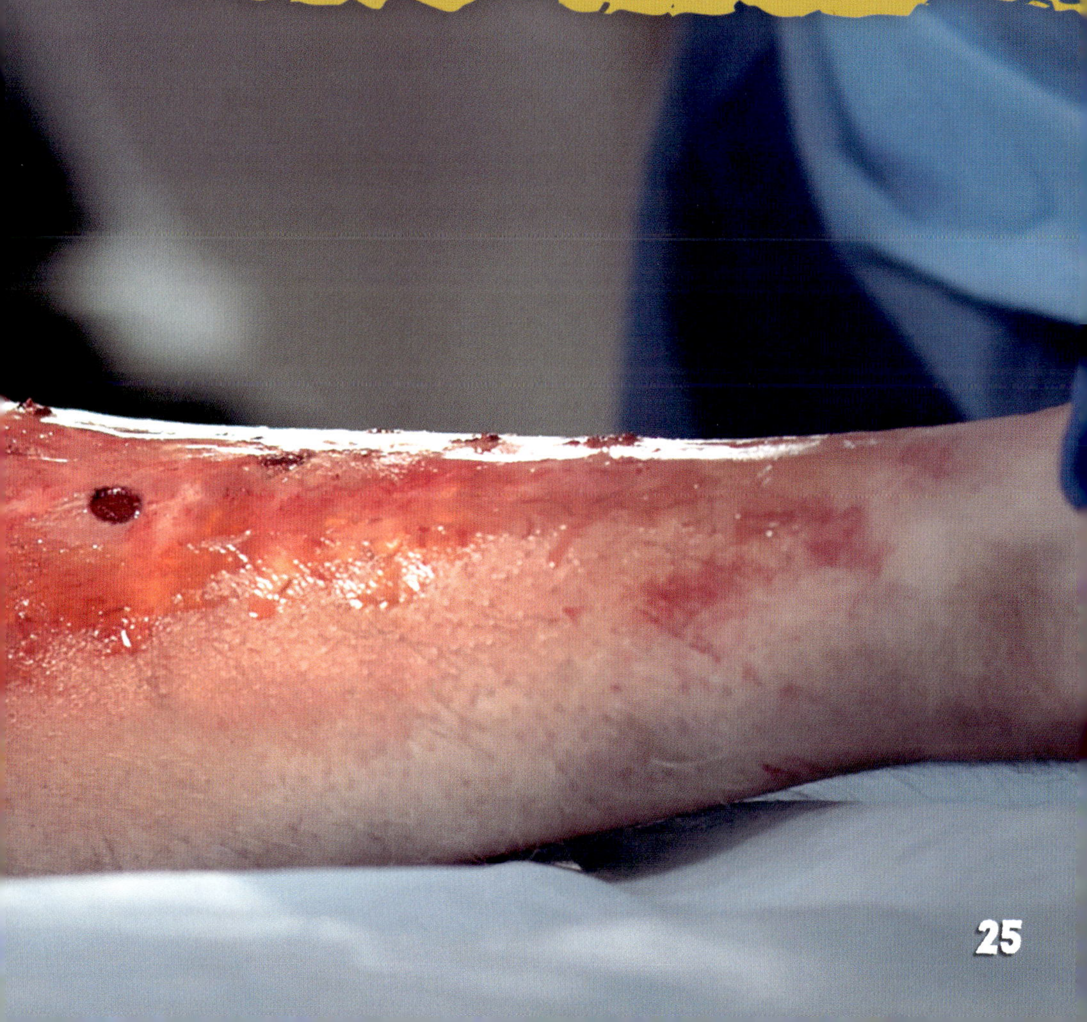

THE CLEAN UP

Primary care doctors try to stop illness before it starts! They offer preventive medicine, such as regular checkups and vaccinations. Caring for the patient is their primary concern!

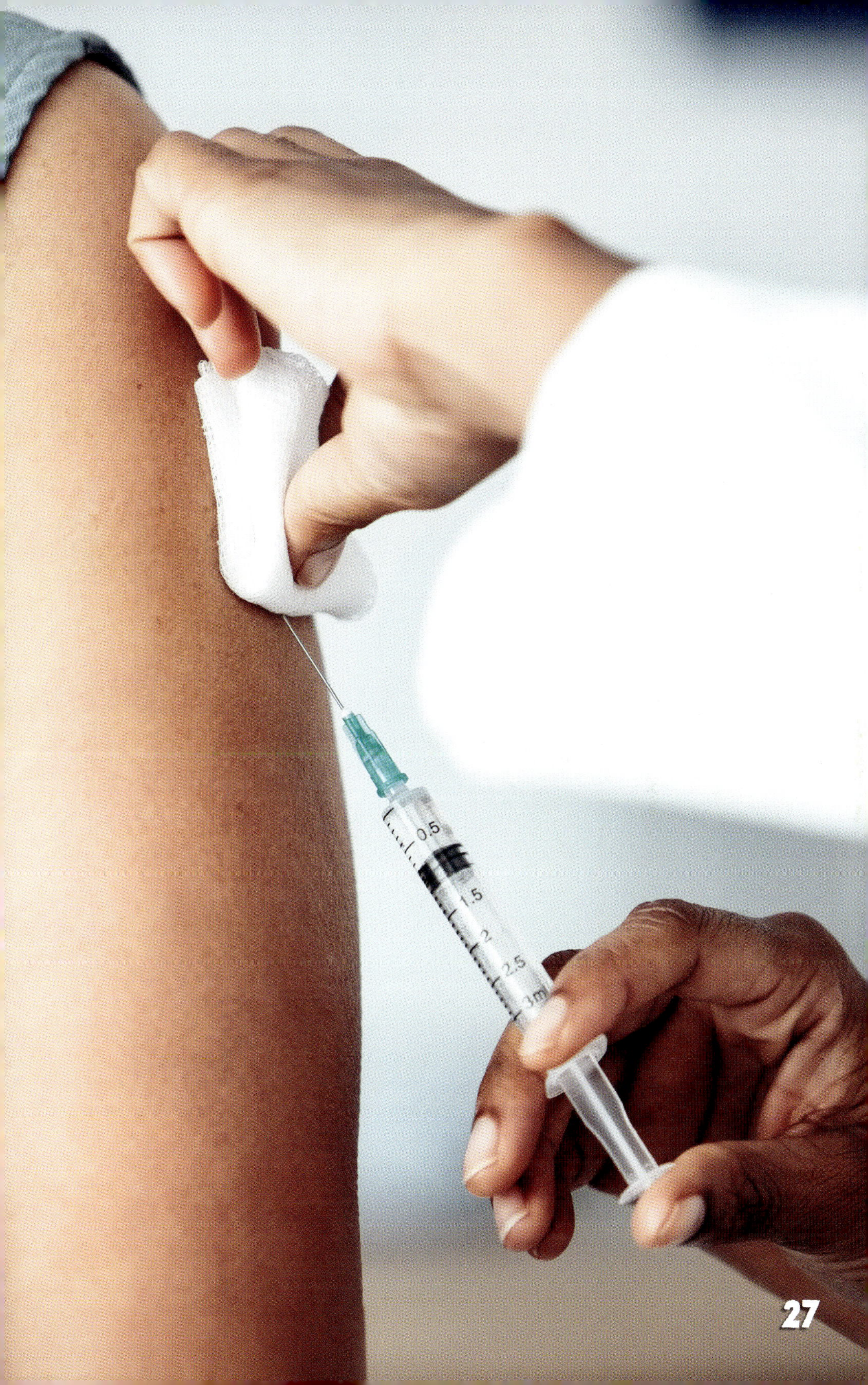
0.5
1.5
2
2.5

Health care jobs come with their fair share of dirt and death. But the workers endure it to save lives and help people feel their best!

GLOSSARY

biohazardous waste – trash that contains harmful germs and viruses. If not handled properly, it can spread diseases.

digestive system – the part of the body that breaks down food, absorbs water, and turns leftovers into poop.

fungal – having to do with fungus.

infection – an illness caused by germs.

ingrown toenail – when a toenail grows into the surrounding skin, causing a painful swelling or redness.

plaque – a film of bacteria and saliva that forms on teeth.

protocol – the proper way of doing something.

sterile – free of living germs and bacteria.

technician – a worker who helps doctors and nurses check a patient's health by using equipment and performing tests.

ulcer – an open sore on the body.

ONLINE RESOURCES

Booklinks
NONFICTION NETWORK
FREE! ONLINE NONFICTION RESOURCES

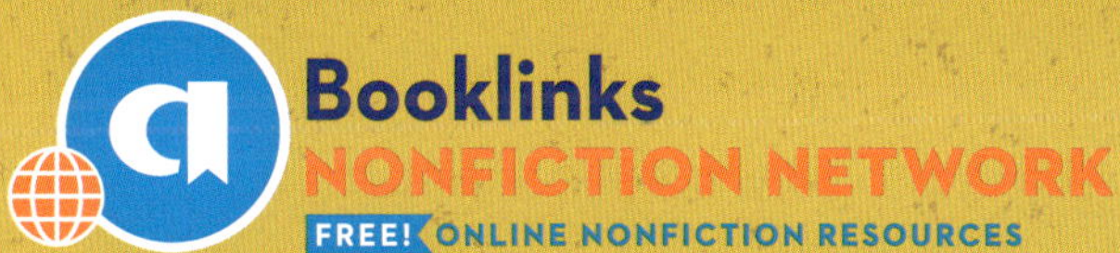

To learn more about dirty health care jobs, please visit abdobooklinks.com or scan this QR code. These links are routinely monitored and updated to provide the most current information available.

INDEX